DATE DUE

D1088191

10/02
DU

AMBULANCES

Please visit our web site at: www.garethstevens.com
For a free color catalog describing Gareth Stevens Publishing's
list of high-quality books and multimedia programs,
call 1-800-542-2595 or fax your request to (414) 332-3567.

Library of Congress Cataloging-in-Publication Data available upon request from publisher.
Fax (414) 336-0157 for the attention of the Publishing Records Department.

ISBN 0-8368-3044-X

First published in 2002 by
Gareth Stevens Publishing
A World Almanac Education Group Company
330 West Olive Street, Suite 100
Milwaukee, WI 53212 USA

Text and photos: Eric Ethan
Cover design and page layout: Tammy Gruenewald

This edition © 2002 by Gareth Stevens, Inc.

Printed in the United States of America

1 2 3 4 5 6 7 8 9 06 05 04 03 02

EMERGENCY VEHICLES

AMBULANCES

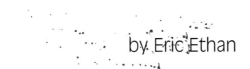

by Eric Ethan

Gareth Stevens Publishing

A WORLD ALMANAC EDUCATION GROUP COMPANY

This is an ambulance. An
ambulance takes people who
are sick or injured to the hospital.

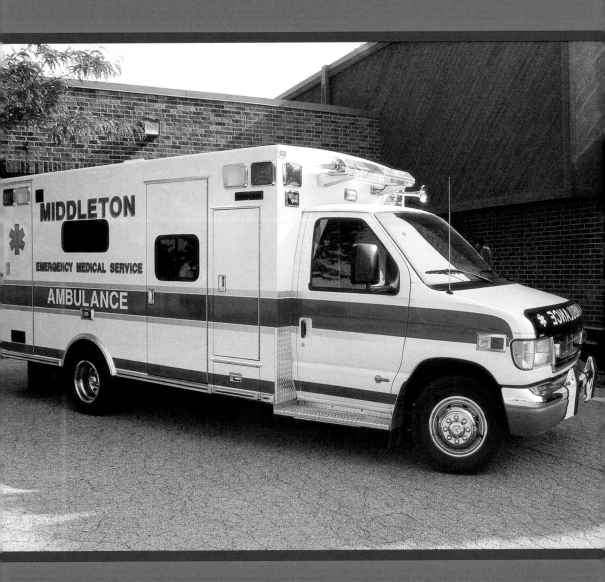

The back of an ambulance has two large doors. These doors make it easy to move a patient in and out of the ambulance.

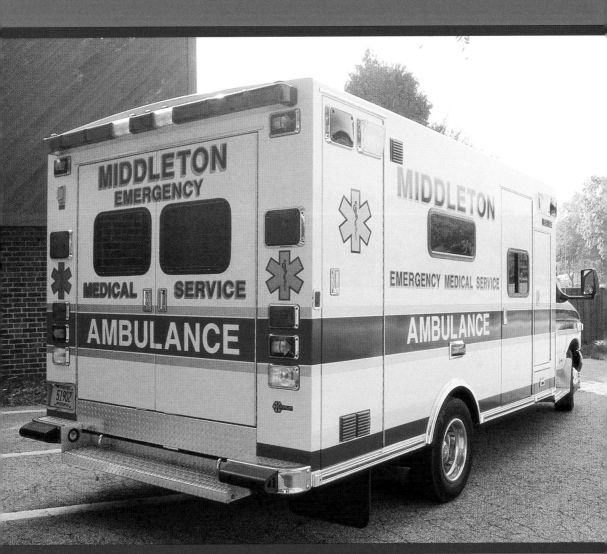

A sick or injured person lies on a stretcher inside the ambulance.

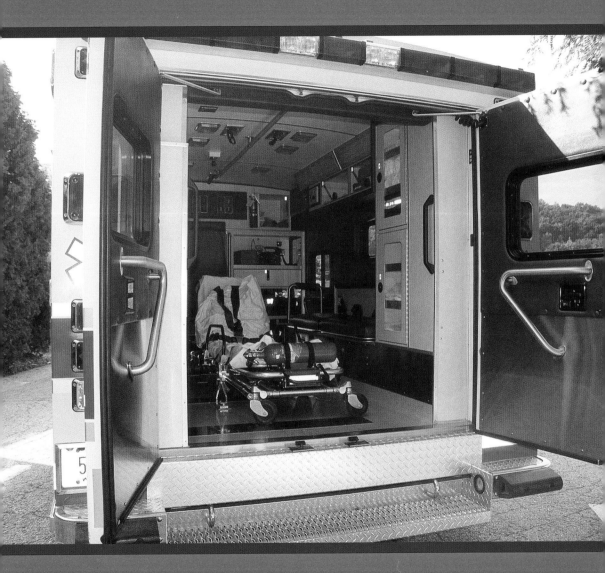

People who work on ambulances are called Emergency Medical Technicians (EMTs).

This chair inside the ambulance can turn all the way around. An EMT sits here to help the person who is sick or hurt.

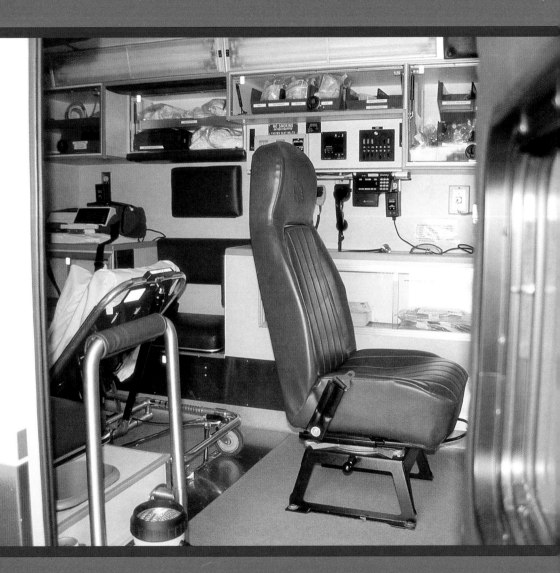

An ambulance has many kinds
of first aid equipment in it. EMTs
are trained to use this equipment.

This EMT is holding an air mask.
An air mask helps a patient breathe.

This EMT is holding equipment that will tell him how a patient is doing. An EMT takes care of a patient all the way to the hospital.

When the next emergency call comes, this ambulance and its crew are ready to go!